HEROES OF HOPE

A collection of
inspirational stories

HEROES OF HOPE

—— A collection of —— inspirational stories

David and Deborah Crone

Published by:

NIS VENTURES INTERNATIONAL

6391 Leisure Town Road, Vacaville, California 95687

Cover by Shelby Gibbs

Graphic Design Shelby Gibbs & Deborah Crone

Printed in The United States of America

Dedication

Deborah and I dedicate Heroes of Hope to family, friends and the real-life people in this book whose lives inspire us and feed our expectation of good.

Acknowledgement

We would like to thank the assistance of Pat Domansky in editing and Shelby Gibbs for her cover and interior contributions. We sincerely thank all those people around the world who have purchased previous books, providing resources for our work in the nations and encouraging us to continue to write. We express a deep love and appreciation for The Mission that has been our extended family for over 26 years.

Contents

Introduction.. 13

The Accountant...................................... 19

The Secret Son...................................... 29

The Conductor...................................... 39

The Young Mill worker............................ 47

The Governor.. 57

The Young Brave Wife............................ 67

The Innkeeper....................................... 75

The Fourth Passenger............................. 83

The Evangelist....................................... 91

The Politician.. 101

The Steadfast Surgeon........................... 109

The Orphans Allies................................. 119

Introduction

I have always been fascinated by stories of historical events and figures. Through my pre-teen and teenage years, it was not unusual for me to read 2 to 3 books a week. The majority of those books were novels set in important times in history with fictional characters interacting with real-ife personalities. My mother would often see the light of my room through the crack at the bottom of the door, knock on the door and remind me that it was time to go to sleep. Just as often I would ignore her reminder and continue to read, sometimes reading by flashlight under my bed covers until late into the night and early morning hours. Even in my high school years I remember sitting in geometry class with The Count of Montecristo attracting my attention much more than the Pythagorean Theorem.

This love for story has continued throughout my life. On any extended vacation, I will read 10 to 15 books, most of which are novels or biographies. It is no surprise that I greatly enjoy the stories found in the Old Testament of Scripture. This attraction to a good story is more than just the enjoyment it provides. Lisa Cron, in her book Wired for Story writes, *"Recent breakthroughs in neuroscience reveal that our brain is hardwired to respond to story; the pleasure we derive from a tale well told is nature's way of seducing us into paying attention to it."* (1)

She goes on to state: *"Thus it's no surprise that when given a choice, people prefer fiction to nonfiction— they'd rather read a historical novel than a history book, watch a movie than a dry documentary. It's not because we're lazy sots but because our neural circuitry is designed to crave story. The rush of intoxication a good story triggers doesn't make us closet hedonists— it makes us willing pupils, primed to absorb the myriad lessons each story imparts."* (1)

Lisa hits directly at the purpose of this book – to stir the reader to be a willing pupil of the lessons hidden for us to find in each story. While I have taken poetic license to create fictional settings to give perspective, the historical context of each story is factual. The primary characters are also real, and true heroes of hope, yet in some stories I have created fictional characters and dialogue that interact with the main character in order to create a window into the authentic context.

The use of fictional settings and characters is not intended to change the factual narrative of the hero's life or contribution. They are simply designed to contribute to an enjoyable experience for the reader, leading to fresh encounters with hope.

The heroes in this collection of inspirational stories are historical or Biblical characters who have lived with hope in challenging times. In doing so, they have inspired hope in the people around them, and made significant contribution to their world and future generations.

David Crone

My hope for you as you read and meditate on these stories is that you become inspired to live your life as a Hero of Hope. As Dave and I researched these amazing people, I became more convinced that these are just normal people who made extraordinary decisions to live in hope.

Heroes are not born; they are created by choices. They are people who choose hope and resist the temptation to bend to circumstances and the opinions of others.

Each of us has the seed of a hero residing inside. Choosing hope gives us the power to become a Hero of Hope for our families, our society, and for generations we will never see.

My heart is filled with the expectation of good for you as you journey into becoming a Hero of Hope.

Deborah Crone

(1) Cron, Lisa. Wired for Story: The Writer's Guide to Using Brain Science to Hook Readers from the Very First Sentence (Introduction). Ten Speed Press. Kindle Edition.

The Accountant

Five hundred *Schindlerjuden* stood in silent reflection over the grave of the flawed, but loved and revered man they knew as Herr Direktor. These five hundred along with countless others scattered throughout Europe, the United States, and Israel owed their very existence to this man that had given away his great wealth to secure their survival. It was with immense gratitude that they stood to honor the only known member of the German Nazi Party to be entombed in Jerusalem on Mount Zion and named "Righteous Among the Nations" by the Israeli government.

The world has been made aware of the remarkable sacrifice of Herr Direktor, Oskar Schindler, through the dramatic novel by Thomas Keneally, *Schindler's Ark* and the film *"Schindler's List"*, adapted from the book by Steven Spielberg. Though Spielberg took Hollywood license in portraying the story of the saving of over 1200 Jews, it is no exaggeration that Schindler gave hope to a people through his dangerous and costly protection of the Jewish employees he loved and for whom he risked his life during the horrors and chaos of WWII.

The accolades and honors bestowed on this Austrian business man by Israel, people around the world, and those he referred to as "my children" are well deserved. Enough could not be said or honor given to a man, who made himself nearly destitute to purchase the survival of individuals and families scheduled for the prison camps and gas chambers of the Nazi Third Reich.

The Jews in the prison camps survived on starvation rations and lived in indescribable filth, experiencing horrific brutality. In contrast, Schindler housed, protected, and fed his Jewish employees, providing 2,000 calories a day for their sustenance at his own expense. He kept families together, provided comfortable accommodations and treated them all with kindness. He spoke courage and gave hope to an otherwise disenfranchised and hopeless people.

Louis Bulow, a Schindler historian, wrote, "Schindler not only saved the lives of 1200 Jews, he saved our faith in humanity..."

Abraham Zuckerman, one of those on the list of Schindler Jews, when commenting on the movie "Schindler's List" stated: "The movie didn't show all the little things he did; he came around and greeted you. I had food, protection, and hope." Abraham is also known to have commented, "To me he was an angel. Because of him I was treated like a human being. And because of him I survived."

Schindler, a wealthy gentile, born to privilege could have lived out his life in luxury in Switzerland, or made his way to the comfort and safety of the United States. Instead, he risked his wealth, his business, and his life for those who would be proud to refer to themselves as the *Schindlerjuden*, "Schindler Jews".

History has given honor to whom honor is due. *And now*, to borrow a famous line from the late commentator Paul Harvey, *the rest of the story.*

It is somewhat likely that the heroic actions of Oskar Schindler and the rescue of over 1,200 lives would not have happened, let alone been told, if it were not for the life and influence of a Jewish accountant by the name of Itzhak Stern, the keeper of *Schindler's list*.

Oskar Schindler first met Itzhak Stern, while seeking financial backing to purchase an enamelware company in Krakow, Poland. The year was 1938 and the company, owned by a consortium of Jewish businessmen, had filed for bankruptcy due to the efforts of those not favorable to Jewish ownership. Oskar had acquired stewardship of the company through bribes, flattery and his connections as a member of the German Military Intelligence Unit, and now wanted to purchase it. Itzhak had the connections Oskar needed.

Itzhak sat silently in his small office looking intently at the man standing on the other side of the desk as if evaluating more than the man's appearance. "I have something to speak to you about Herr Stern " Schindler boldly began to speak as Itzhak motioned for him to be seated.

Taking the offered chair, Oskar was confident he could persuade the accountant to accept his offer and boldly continued without waiting to be invited. "I believe you and I could make a great partnership. With my business connections and your finances, we could turn a mediocre factory into an extremely profitable business."

Itzhak, not blind to the character and history of the man sitting in front of him, continued to silently evaluate Oskar and considered the offer. Looking beyond Schindler's bluster, Itzhak began to identify something in Oskar that many others had not. "I find the proposition interesting." He spoke, breaking his silence, "Please tell me more."

Schindler didn't hesitate and quickly and thoroughly laid out his plan for the development and expansion of the enamelware company. As Itzhak listened to the man's vision, a confidence rose in his heart that at the core, Oskar Schindler was "a good German". This hope that there was something worth rescuing in his potential new business partner guided him to agree to assist Oskar.

Itzhak and Oskar could not have been more opposite. Itshak, a Jew, was born into a strong moral and religious family that instilled in him that faith and culture. He was an accountant that spent his life serving the ambitions of others and had a love for his people that guided many of his choices.

Oskar, the man Itzhak met in 1938 was not the man he would become. Oscar had been born into the privileged upper class and took advantage of the corruptive potential that the privilege afforded. Known to be a self-centered, womanizing, and unprincipled man, Oskar had little or no moral compass. He was an ambitious and opportunistic business man unafraid of methods less than integrase or ethical, and as such joined the Nazi Party for the benefits it provided in the depression years prior to WWII.

Itzhak Sterns hope that there was something in Schindler that could be redeemed and used for good did more than cause him to go into business with Oskar. His belief in the man led Itzhak to use his influence to aid the evolution of a war-profiteer into the deliverer of Jews.

Schindler often commented about the difficult days in which

they lived. On one such occasion he referred to them as a time when life did not have "the value of a pack of cigarettes". Stern used the opportunity to quote the Talmudic verse: "He who saves one life, it is as if he has saved the entire world." Though Schindler shrugged the quote off with a brusque comment, "Of course, of course", Itzhak knew he had planted a seed that would aid Schindler's transformation.

The influence of Stern on Schindler's thinking and values set Oskar up for the defining moments when he would witness the brutality of the Aktionen. The Aktionen was a cruel and ferocious round up of Jews out of the ghettos by the Nazi's for deportation to the death camps. The violent, inhuman treatment of men, women and children ruthlessly being herded onto the trains sickened Schindler.

Each time he witnessed this atrocity, Oskar moved closer to the "Good German" Itzhak always believed him to be. "Beyond this day," referring to one of these strikes, Schindler reflected, "no thinking person could fail to see what would happen. I was now resolved to do everything in my power to defeat the system."

It was Stern who engineered the strategy to help protect fellow Jews by bringing them into the factory as forced labor. He informed Schindler that Jewish slave labor was less costly than Polish labor and would continue to encourage him to hire more Jews. In so doing, Stern and Oskar secured their safety, and Stern brought Oskar into contact with the plight of Sterns people.

This exposure to Stern and the Jews in his factory began to shift the value Oskar had for these people. He would no longer see them as chattel to be used and discarded but as human beings with dignity and worth.

Abraham Zuckerman shares the following when recalling the day Schindler rescued 300 women heading to the gas chamber in the Auschwitz death camp:

"What people don't understand about Oscar is the power of the man, his strength, his determination. Everything he did he did to save the Jews. Can you imagine what power it took for him to pull out from Auschwitz 300 people? At Auschwitz, there was only one way you got out, we used to say. Through the chimney! Understand? Nobody ever got out of Auschwitz. But Schindler got out 300 ...! "

It is fitting that Oskar Schindler was honored on April 28th, 1962, with the title of Righteous Gentile. It is appropriate that he has been given a prominent place in the Yad Vishim Memorial in Jerusalem, where the six million Jews that were exterminated in the war are honored.

It is only right, as well, that 500 *Schindler Jews*, gathered to memorialize him as he was buried on Mount Zion. To millions he is a deliverer and to the estimated 8,500 descendants of Schindler Jews scattered around the world, he is the man who made possible their very existence.

It is interesting to note that most of those 500 *Schindlerjuden* standing around Schindler's grave, also stood beside the burial place of Itzhak Stern five years earlier. As they honored the accountant that day, they watched Oskar Schindler, the man who knew the rest of the story, weep like a child as he said farewell to his friend and partner.

As we honor one who has deserved such honor, let's not forget the man, who by hope-filled influence, encouraged the transformation of Oskar Schindler from a lost soul, to the savior of a generation - Itzhak Stern, the accountant, and keeper of Schindler's list.

Oskar Schindler and Itzhak Stern, a Gentile and a Jew, both Heroes of Hope.

Thoughts

The Secret Son

The young mother knew she could never openly reveal her secret. Only her husband and two other children would know of the son she birthed at such a difficult time. But that was not the only sadness that overshadowed her as she went about her daily responsibilities and prayed that the little one would not be discovered by the neighbors or the authorities. As she looked down on her 3-month-old son reflecting on the events of the last year, she knew that the day was fast approaching when she might lose him forever.

Though Jochebed and her husband Amram had been content raising their young son and his older sister, the news that they were expecting another child was not completely unwelcomed. They had often talked of another child, but usually left those conversations troubled by the potential ramifications. Now that they knew a child was on its way, they had to face the reality that their hope for the child in Jochebed's womb could be crushed under the oppressive government that did not want any more male children born of their ethnicity.

"They've taken my son." The anguished cry from outside their modest home startled Jochebed from her thoughts as she was preparing the evening meal. She recognized the voice of her closest friend as the words registered in her mind and struck terror in her heart. The now heartbroken mother had given birth to a son just a few days before; and though the couple had hidden the child, someone must have revealed their hiding place.

"They've taken him, Jochebed." her friend sobbed as she stumbled through the door and fell into Jochebed's arms. The look of anguish and pain on her friends face as Jochebed tried to comfort her was a picture she would never forget. It would linger in her thoughts for the rest of her pregnancy and the months that would follow. Would the pain of her friend be hers too?

Then the day came when the birth pains began and Jochebed went to hide herself in a prearranged location in a cave near their home. It was a place known by other mothers like herself, who needed to give birth in secret. Their daughter ran to get Puah, a trusted midwife, as Amram continued to go about his day as if nothing was happening so as to not alert the authorities.

Never had joyful anticipation been so mixed with concern as Jochebed pushed to release the child from her womb. Puah watched as the head and shoulders of the child broke through. One more push and they would know.

Puah knew what her instructions were from the government. She was also aware of the deadly consequences to her own life if she didn't follow through with the official order. This was not the first time she was faced with the conflict between the law and her conscience and would not be the last. Puah, however, had long since set her heart to do all she could to protect every child, whether male or female.

The infant's cry did not reveal the answer to the question foremost in Jochebed's mind, but the concern on Puah's face told her all she needed to know – a son. "Is he healthy?" was her first inquiry. "Oh yes, a very healthy boy", replied the midwife. "A son you and Amram can be proud of." The emotions of living in the hope of a son and the fear of its reality crashed in on Jochebed, and she began to weep.

Jochebed's daughter, Miriam, having been tending the fire outside the makeshift shelter came running as she heard the baby's cry. She arrived at her mother's side just as her mother's crying joined that of her new brother.

Miriam quietly consoled her mother as she wiped the perspiration from her forehead. "You have always reminded me that Jehovah is our provider", Miriam stated confidently, "and he will help us find a way."

"And find a way He did," Jochebed whispered in reflection. She remembered how she and Amram had hidden the child, placing their faith in Jehovah, hoping that their son would have a future. It hadn't been easy to disguise the sound of an infant's cry or the family activities essential for caring for a new baby. There were many times when their hearts nearly stopped, thinking their secret had been discovered.

Each day Jochebed's heart was increasingly knit to the heart of her son as she sheltered, fed and held him in her arms. Now, as she sat next to her son watching him sleep, Jochebed knew the time was close when she must find another way to care for their son before he was discovered.

Jochebed had often found comfort in Jehovah, and now she needed not only comfort but a new strategy. She found a secluded place in the corner of her home and quietly, but earnestly prayed. "Jehovah, you have been our provider and protection. You have kept our son safe these months, and I ask that you help me again to know what to do. I trust you and place my hope in your wisdom and power."

Jochebed didn't know if she had heard a voice or had an impression, but as she stood up from her time of prayer, she was certain of what to do. "Miriam" she cried, calling her daughter in from outside. "Gather some reeds from the river and bring them to me." When Miriam hesitated, looking at her mother with questioning eyes, Jochebed prodded, "Quickly, go, now!"

As Jochebed watched Miriam hurry toward the river, hope was filling her heart. She had no idea what the future would look like for the child; she only knew that God had given her a plan.

The next day the family gathered around the papyrus basket

Jochebed had weaved out of the reeds Miriam had collected. Tears ran down each of their faces as they kissed his cheek and said a prayer for his safety. Jochebed then wrapped her son in a soft Hebrew weaved cloth and laid him gently into the basket.

Fearing they would be discovered, Amram, and his older son Aaron stayed back at the house as Jochebed and Miriam made the brief journey to the river, carrying the child in the basket. Once there, Jochebed instructed Miriam to find a place off in the distance where she could observe her brother without being discovered.

With hope overriding her apprehension and sorrow, Jochebed placed the ark among the reeds along the shore. As she turned from the river and began the lonely walk back to her home, Jochebed whispered through her tears, "Jehovah, you are my hope. I release my son into your care."

Miriam watched with concern from her hiding place as a beautifully dressed bather approached the reeds where the basket floated. Miriam's concern grew into near panic as she realized the cry of her brother had attracted the woman away from her normal place of bathing, and to this part of the river.

Following the sound, the woman of obvious wealth, came to the heavy reeds along the shore and spotted the basket. As the woman investigated the baskets content, she discovered the infant. With curiosity and concern, she reached in and lifted the baby to her chest. It was then that she noticed the weave of the cloth that surrounded the child – the weave of the Hebrew slaves. Now, the daughter of Pharaoh, like Jochebed, had a secret she could never openly reveal.

The epic story of the deliverance of Israel from slavery in Egypt could never have happened if not for the courageous lives of several key characters. Each of them played their role as Heroes of hope.

One of the characters without whose hope and courage this story would not have happened has her name recorded in scripture. This hope carrier is Puah, the midwife. Puah is one of the many Hebrew midwives who were courageous enough to refuse to follow the king's edict and wise enough to escape his wrath. Their actions in rescuing newborn male children gave hope to all expectant mothers.

Another character important to this story is the daughter of Pharaoh, whose name is only conjecture. In spite of her father's decree to kill all the male Hebrew children, this courageous woman rescued the infant; adopted, named, and raised him under the very shadow of Pharaoh's wrath.

Above all are the two main characters in this Heroes of Hope story: Jochebed and Amram, the blood parents of the deliverer, Moses. They along with those mentioned above, were amazing people, especially when you consider the times and conditions in which they lived.

Under the favor granted Joseph, the son of the Hebrew Jacob and an influential ruler in Egypt, the children of Israel multiplied and prospered. They so flourished that they outnumbered the Egyptians in population.

After the death of Joseph and all his generation, a Pharaoh came to power that didn't know Joseph and feared the growing influence of the Jews. In order to control them, He began a process of taking them from freedom into forced labor and slavery.

The people of Israel however did not weaken under slavery, but grew stronger. This caused even greater fear among the Egyptians, and they increased their oppression of the Jews.

The King, desiring to deplete the population of Hebrew males, commanded all the Hebrew midwives to kill every son born to a Jew at the time of birth. When the midwives ignored the kings command, Pharaoh decreed that all Egyptians were required to kill every newborn Hebrew male, essentially creating a genocidal nation.

In this culture of tyranny and death, Jochebed and Amram conceived a son. Jochebed carried, birthed, and protected the child that would become the deliverer of a nation.
It is no wonder that Jochebed and Amram are listed in the great hall of faith found in the book of Hebrews. They along with Puah the midwife and Pharaohs daughter are true courageous Heroes of hope, who partnered with God to answer the cry of His people.

Thoughts

The Conductor

Minty aimed the gun with intent at the head of the troublesome man and said, "You go on or die." The man looked along the short barrel of the pistol and into her eyes, calculating the woman's resolve. As if perceiving his uncertainty, she slowly pulled back the hammer and repeated, "You go on or die".

The men, women and children watching the scene unfold in front of them huddled closer together and prayed that the man would come to his senses and choose to go on. His life, and theirs depended on it. None of them questioned what Minty would do, for they had heard the stories.

The man, now convinced of Minty's dogged determination slowly backed away, turned and walked down the trail. Minty lowered the revolver, collected her other charges, and led them toward the next stop along the Underground Railroad.

This was not the first time, nor would it be the last that Minty would have to threaten one of her passengers to keep them from endangering everyone by trying to return to the perceived security of their owners. The road from slavery to freedom was never without its problems, but this trip had been unusually filled with difficulties: cold, hunger, crippling fear of being discovered, and the terror of the unknown. All of these realities brought out the best and worst in those risking their life for the hope of a better one.

As Minty followed the eighteen slaves along the trail in the dark, she began to reflect on her life and the journey that led her to take on the task of helping slaves escape their owners and find a new life in the North.

Born into a slave family in Maryland, as Araminta Ross, somewhere around the year 1822, Minty would learn the horrors and brutality of slavery first hand. Whipped often as a child, she would bear the scars on her body the rest of her life. When still young she received a blow to the head by a metal object, thrown by her owner that left her with headaches that troubled her until her death.

Growing into a woman within the slave culture Minty became passionate about two things that would guide her life: a hatred for the indignity of slavery and a fervent faith in God. The first fostered by what she saw and experienced around her, and the second, cultivated by the faith of her mother, who often read Bible stories to her.

Shortly before Minty married John, a free black man, she was to be sold and separated from her family. Instead of waiting for this to happen she decided to escape with her two brothers. "There was one of two things I had a right to," she explained later, "liberty or death; if I could not have one, I would have the other."

Minty's freedom would be short lived as her brothers became fearful of being caught and punished and chose to return to their masters. Minty, not wanting to abandon her family, did the same. Upon returning to her slave existence, Minty married John. But her passion for freedom would not leave her and she again, escaped to the North never to be owned by anyone again.

Upon crossing into the free state of Pennsylvania, Minty would later recall: "When I found I had crossed that line, I looked at my hands to see if I was the same person. There was such a glory over everything; the sun came like gold through the trees, and over the fields, and I felt like I was in Heaven."

It would have been prudent for Minty to find her way into some faraway place and remain safe from the possibility of recapture. However, her hatred of slavery and desire to see the rest of her family and other slaves find freedom, overcame fear for her own life; and she became active in helping in the underground railroad.

Over the next fifteen years following Minty's escape to the north, the woman better known as Harriet Tubman, would help many of her family members and others escape to freedom. She personally conducted over 300 runaway slaves to safety along the Underground Railway.

The underground railroad, formed in the late 1700's, got its name from the terms used to describe the people, places and routs used to help slaves escape into free states and Canada. Abolitionists like Harriet who helped in the railroad were called conductors; the safe houses along the route were referred to as stations or depots.

The conductor would lead the freed slaves from station to station by traveling at night and hiding in the day. One estimate suggests that by 1850, 100,000 slaves had been led to freedom in this way.

After the passage of the Fugitive Slave Law of 1850, which allowed the recapture of slaves found living in the north, Harriet began taking the slaves into the Canadian Territory. Her herculean efforts earned her the nickname of "Moses," and she would use a version of the song "Go down Moses" to signal her charges.

The journey to freedom was never easy, at times having to hide herself and her charges in holes in the ground to keep from being detected. Not being able to read, she never understood the wanted posters, offering as much as $40,000.00 dollars for her apprehension, dead or alive. In spite of the many difficulties and dangers, this Moses like her namesake was a true deliverer. Here in her own words:

I wuz de conductor ob de Underground' Railway an " I kin say what mos' conductors can't say—dat I nebber run my train off de track an' I nebber los' a passenger.

Harriet's work as an abolitionist didn't stop with her work in the railroad. When the civil war began, she joined the Union Army. At first she worked as a cook and a nurse. It wasn't long, however, until her superiors recognized her leadership ability and she was given the responsibility of scouting and spying on the Southern army.

Guided by visions and dreams, she believed to come from God, Harriet had an uncanny way of knowing things others didn't. Her leadership was so highly regarded she became the first woman to lead an armed expedition in the Civil war. That expedition in South Carolina liberated more than 700 slaves.

Following the end of the civil war, Harriet remained active in civil rights causes and women's suffrage. This great woman of hope ceased her labor and passed from this world in 1913, while living in a rest home named in her honor. That would not be the last honor that would be paid this underground railroad conductor. Schools across the nation bear her name, and in 1944, a liberty ship was named after her. A US postage stamp bears her image, and in 2013, the Harriet Tubman Underground Railroad National Monument was begun.

There are many other honors that have been given to Harriet (Minty) Tubman since her death, including plans to have her image grace the front of the twenty-dollar bill. The greatest honor, however, will best be told by the thousands of lives she helped set free, including the slave that had the wisdom to "go on" instead of testing Minty's resolve.

As Harriet lay weak with pneumonia, knowing that she was about to take her last breath, the conductor, this Hero of Hope, that had given courage to so many gave her final directive to those who surrounded her bed: "I go to prepare a place for you." It was what she had done all her adult life, and it's only fitting that she continues in life after death.

Thoughts

The Young Mill Worker

David fell onto the bed completely exhausted from the long grueling hours of labor at the mill in his hometown of Blantyre, Lanarkshire, Scotland. At the age of eleven, David was already a veteran employee of the mill, having started when he was ten, due to the needs of his poverty-stricken family.

Every day was the same in young David's life – and would be for the next fourteen years. He would get up before the sun was evident in the sky, labor wearisome hours at the mill, and return home after the sun had dropped below the horizon.

This existence was not the life that young David had hoped for. It certainly did not answer the longing that had slowly crept into his heart and was increasingly capturing his thoughts and dreams. As David fell off to sleep, he whispered what he so often wondered on the other countless nights like this one; "Am I dreaming an impossible dream."

David's vision beyond the mill was not fueled by a desire to escape hard work, for his father, a Sunday school teacher in the village protestant church, had instilled in him the importance of a strong work ethic as well as the value of faith. David's aspiration for his future came instead from his love of science and exploration. Each night after the hours at the mill, he would study geology, the natural world, and other sciences as well as religion. He dreamt of exploring unexplored places and bringing aid to those in need of hope.

David would eventually break free from the mill; and at the age of twenty-six, he entered Anderson's College in Glasgow, training as a medical missionary. Upon completion of his course, David secured passage to Africa and began working among the natives and exploring the region. When being questioned on the wisdom of his choice, He stated:

> "Cannot the love of Christ carry the missionary where the slave-trade carries the trader? I shall open up a path to the interior or perish."

Another young boy, John, also had his dreams, dreams of replacing his life in the workhouse with a new one somewhere else in the world. As with David, every day was the same for this teenage boy - hard work and little to look forward to. As he lay on the bed he had slept on since he was five years old, his vision was fueled by the desire to escape the memories of an alcoholic father and a prostitute mother.

John had a passion to be something better than his heritage. After being released from the workhouse at the age of fifteen, he changed his name to Henry and went out into the world to prove to himself and the world that he was a man worth believing in. He moved to America, fought on both sides of the American civil war, then became a journalist covering the American Indian wars. At the age of 28, Henry had become known as a brash cigar-smoking reporter for the New York Herald. He was ready for any great adventure.

David Livingstone and Henry Stanley were two men on a collision course with destiny, whose names would be forever linked in history.

David Livingstone, the once young boy asleep on his bed dreaming of the potential of his future, would soon discover that the road that leads to the reality of things hoped for is never simply handed to a person. Its realization requires a willingness to engage the impossible and fight through the opposing circumstances.

The years between that eleven-year-old hope-filled mill worker and the man who would one day be recognized as one of the greatest missionaries and explorer of our time were not easy ones. For David Livingstone, they were filled with disappointment, illness and opposition. David admitted to this when he wrote in one of his last journals, "It is not all pleasure, this exploration."

One of David's fellow physicians, John Kirk once said of Dr. Livingstone, "I can come to no other conclusion than that Dr. Livingstone is out of his mind and a most unsafe leader." It is interesting to note that very few, if any, can recall the accomplishments of John Kirk, while David Livingstone has been universally acclaimed for his work as both a missionary and explorer.

It was Dr. Livingston not Dr. Kirk that walked where no white man had previously placed his foot; discovered the waterfall Mosi-oa-Tunya; would rename Victoria Falls, help provoke public support against slavery; and make the first successful transcontinental journey across Africa while declaring the life-giving message of the love of God.

Once, when offered help with his work in Africa, he replied:

> "If you have men who will only come if they
> know there is a good road, I don't want them,
> I want men who will come if there is no road
> at all."

Many years after David's first incursion into the interior of Africa and nearly 4 years before his death, Henry Stanley, the brash correspondent from the New York Herald chose to go where there was no road.

Henry had been sent by his editor, James Bennett Jr. to determine the death of Dr. Livingstone. Bennett avidly disliked the British and hoped that Stanley, thought to be an American, would discover Livingston, where the British had failed. What Bennett was unaware of was that Stanley's real name was John Rowlands and he was born in Denbigh, Wales.

It seems that Stanley took the discovery of Livingstone, alive or dead, personally. Though he greatly feared the dark continent, Henry refused to give up his search in spite of bouts of malaria, dysentery, and facing starvation. He wrote to his editor the following statement of resolve:

"Until I hear more of him or see the long absent old man face to face, I bid you a farewell," he signed off. "But wherever he is, be sure I shall not give up the chase. If alive you shall hear what he has to say. If dead, I will find him and bring his bones to you."

Henry Stanley did indeed find Dr. Livingstone. He located him November 10, 1871, in the town of Ujiji on the shores of Lake Tanganyika. It had been 6 years since anyone had heard from David. Stanley found the missionary looking pale and frail with white hair, a busy beard and missing teeth.

With the honor due the man that stood before him, Henry walked up to David and greeted him with the now famous refrain: "Dr. Livingstone I presume?"

Upon David's positive reply Stanly exclaimed, "I thank God, doctor, I have been permitted to see you." Where upon David Livingstone replied, "Yes, and I feel thankful that I am here to welcome you."

Eighteen months after that historic meeting on a hot and humid day in 1873, David Livingstone knelt to pray in the village of LLala, Zambia. Neither the circumstances nor the action were unusual, but it would be the last time David would kneel. As he prayed, the internal bleeding caused by dysentery and the malaria that had so often attacked him, took their final toll on David's body and he died. The carving in the tree at the site of his death cites the date as May 4th.

Henry Stanley was so inspired by the character and passion of his new friend that following David's Death, Henry came back to Africa and continued David's exploration. His name now graces cities and waterways in that continent.

David's influence left a lasting mark on Henry. Upon leaving Africa and returning to England, the man whose name was once John Rowlands became Sir Henry Stanley. The illegitimate son of a drunkard and a prostitute became a member of Parliament and was made a Knight Grand Cross of the Order of the Bath.

Henry Morton died on May 10, 1904. Etched on a piece of granite that marks his grave is the epithet, "Henry Morton Stanley, Bula Matari," translated "Breaker of Rocks". Bula Matari was the name given to Stanly by the natives of the Congo.

David Livingstone, the hope-filled young dreamer growing up in Scotland came to capture the heart of a continent. The greatest testimony of this reality is found in the actions of the Africans whose lives Dr. Livingstone impacted. Upon his death, the natives carried his body to the coast to be shipped back to England, where David would receive the high honor of being buried in West Minster Abbey. However, before they transported his body, they removed his heart and buried it in African soil under a tree near the place of his death, declaring:

"You can have his body, but his heart belongs in Africa!"

Though a life of hope cannot be summed up in one quote, the following comes close:

> "I place no value on anything I have or may possess, except in relation to the kingdom of God. If anything will advance the interests of the kingdom, it shall be given away or kept, only as by giving or keeping it I shall most promote the glory of Him to whom I owe all my hopes in time or eternity."
> — David Livingstone

Thoughts

The Governor

As the sun kissed the horizon, the young assistant stood holding the reigns of the governors' horse while gazing with admiration at the man responsible for completing the project in 52 days. No one believed the undertaking the governor was now surveying could be done at all, let alone in the short time span of under two months. Nathan had been one of those that dismissed the idea. There was too much oppression by their enemies, Nathan had reasoned, and too much apathy among the people for anything as significant as what now lay before them to be accomplished.

The people of this too often invaded province had lost all hope of ever recovering the glory and influence of the land they often heard described by their elders. The stories told by parents and grandparents were the history of this generation and not at all their present reality. Though they had returned to the land after decades of absence with great expectation of restoring their lives and their destiny, little over the last several years bolstered their dreams. Circumstances, disappointments, and continued opposition had stolen their hope and left them apathetic to their condition.

As Nathan continued to be mesmerized by the scene before him, his thoughts took him to the day everything began to change and hope was given a chance to grow. In the early morning hours of that significant day, a messenger rode into the city and announced that the new governor and his entourage would arrive later that afternoon. A cautious excitement spread throughout the city, and people began to line the streets in anticipation of the appearance of the Kings emissary.

Nathan was more than just one of those interested onlookers that watched as the governor, along with a troop of captains and their horsemen approached the city. He had been chosen by the city elders to be part of the official welcoming committee. Nathan watched in rapt attention as the representatives of the King rode through the broken down and burned gate that had at one time welcomed visitors and citizens alike with royal splendor. Sadly, on that day, as the regal party entered the city, the gates were a dismal reflection of a day long gone.

Yet, as Nathan considered that day and all that had transpired since, he was nearly overwhelmed by the emotions of joy and the expectation of things to come.

The governor, like Nathan, well remembered the day of his arrival in the province. He had quickly recognized the tragic state of the city and the distressed condition of its people long before entering the gates. However, as he stood with Nathan looking over the city, his thoughts were not on that day but on the day long before, when his own indifference was challenged and hope for himself and his people was ignited.

He was not a governor then but held high office in the court of the king. His position was one of great trust and influence and he enjoyed the benefits that his office afforded. He was in fact, a servant, yet he lived more like a King. He was housed in luxurious accommodations, ate the best cuisine a king's table could provide, and was allowed the liberties very few enjoyed. Though he was not of the same faith as his king, he had been allowed to worship his God and practice the lifestyle of his beliefs.

The man who would one day govern a poor and oppressed province was content living in the land of his birth with affluence and privilege. He not only had lived far from the people of that province geographically, but distant from them in his daily thoughts. All that, however, changed the day the Jew Hanani arrived at the fortified palace of Shushan, and Nehemiah, the cupbearer to the King of Babylon made what seemed to be an innocent inquiry. Little did know he know that the answer to his question would alter his destiny and the plight of his people well beyond his lifetime.

"Hanani, many of our people have left this land they were born in and returned to Jerusalem. Are they doing well in their new land and new freedom?" Nehemiah asked his guest more out of curiosity than genuine concern, having no idea the deep-seated emotion the answer would evoke. "And what about the city? How is its condition now that the people have returned?"

Hanani's response was measured, yet tinged with passion; "The survivors," he began, with tears filling his eyes, "have returned to Jerusalem from decades of captivity and are greatly suffering. They live under constant accusation and criticism from the people around them and are treated as strangers in a land once their own."

Hanani's tears where now flowing down his cheeks and onto the floor as he began to describe his beloved Jerusalem. "The city is still in ruins and the gates have been burned. The once great walls of the city are broken down, leaving rubble everywhere." Hanani's emotions were now nearly uncontrolled as he spoke again of his people, "Nehemiah, our people are lost, and their hope is gone."

The passion of Hanani's description pierced deep into the heart of Nehemiah. He attempted to shut down his emotions while he listened to Hanani's narrative; but with every word he became increasingly overwhelmed with a deep sense of sorrow and responsibility.

As Hanani continued to recount the dilapidated condition of the once great city of Jerusalem and the hopelessness of its people, the sorrow building up inside of Nehemiah became so great that he collapsed in his chair weeping. Hanani tried to continue with his story, but Nehemiah's raised his hand to stop him, and through his tears asked him to leave his chamber.

Nehemiah mourned and wept for many days, never leaving his room, eating nothing, and spending his time praying.
It was in those days of deep sorrow and repentance that Nehemiah realized he could no longer ignore the condition of his people, and a plan was birthed in his heart. It was a plan to rebuild the walls of Jerusalem and establish a government that would bring hope to the people of Jerusalem and re-establish the identity of the nation of Israel.

Nehemiah knew that for his plan to be successful, it would require the permission and authority of the king. He also was certain that his request could be so offensive to the King that his own life would be in danger. It was with this understanding in mind, that Nehemiah sought the favor of God.

"Oh Jehovah, please listen to my request and the request of those who take pleasure in honoring your name. Grant me, your servant, success this day by giving me favor before the King."

As Nehemiah thought back on those days, he mounted his horse, and with Nathan riding beside him took the trail down into the city. "Nathan," he said, "Never give up hope, for your hope is important for everyone around you." Nathan gazed at the governor and nodded in understanding.

The book of Nehemiah records that Nehemiah's prayer was answered, and King Artaxerxes not only allowed Nehemiah to go to Jerusalem but gave him full authority and financial support for the rebuilding of the wall. Though Nehemiah faced difficult opposition from those threatened by the resurgence of Jerusalem, the wall was rebuilt and the gates hung – all in a miraculous 52 days.

Nehemiah's journal is truly the story of hope coming to a hopeless people. To understand the import and impact of the rebuilding of the wall a little history is necessary.

Approximately a hundred and seventy years before Nehemiah left Babylon and entered the city of Jerusalem, the nation of Israel was overrun by the Babylonians and its people, over two million, were taken captive to Babylon. Twenty years later, the city and temple of Jerusalem was destroyed and left in ruins. By the time Nehemiah put his plan to rebuild the walls into action, the walls of the city had been in rubble for over one hundred and fifty years.

The captivity of Israel lasted seventy years, at the end of which the Jews were allowed to return home. By this time most had made their homes in Babylon; and out of the more than 2 million that were taken from Palestine, no more that 50,000 chose to return.

Later, under the leadership of the prophet Ezra, the temple was rebuilt; and seventy-five years before the writing of the book of Nehemiah, an effort to rebuild the walls began. That effort, however, failed under the weight of tremendous opposition by enemies that, in the absence of the Jews, had established their own communities.

It is easy to understand, with this history in mind, how important the work of Nehemiah was to the people of Jerusalem. An un-walled city was a city without protection. This left its inhabitants at the mercy of local warlords, and open to the takeover of enemy armies. Every progress made to establish order and government was easily destroyed, and any effort to improve the condition of the people became wasted effort. Though Jerusalem was under the rule of Babylon, its welfare was of little concern to that great nation.

These impossible conditions had been the reality of the people of Jerusalem for 100 years. The people had grown complacent and without vision, caught in a victim culture without hope. But God was not blind to their condition and he prepared and sent a man so captivated by the expectation of good that betrayal, treachery, deceit and threat could not derail him from his mission.

Nehemiah, a true Hero of Hope, built a wall – but so much more. Out of the rubble of a ruined city and a broken people, a stronghold of hope emerged, and order, identity, and destiny were restored.

Thoughts

The Young Brave Wife

The young mother was saddened though not surprised by the soulful inquiry of her young son as he stood in front of the window of the only home he had known. Mother Edi had been aware since shortly after her son's birth that he would be required to see life uniquely, that blindness would eventually darken his world. The pain of that truth never fully left her thoughts and often pushed her emotions to the edge of pity for her and her husband's much-loved boy.

"When I am older" her son inquired, "will I see Poldo's house?" This was not the first time nor would it be the last that Edi would have to weigh her answer and choose between an easy response that spoke false expectation and a truthful one that offered genuine hope. As difficult as these moments were for Edi, her response had been determined years before, tempered in the heat of potential tragedy.

Edi and Alessandro loved their life, working the family farm in a rural village in the beautiful region of Tuscany, Italy, and anticipating the birth of their child. What they didn't expect was the pain Edi began to experience in her lower right side that continued to increase until she was hospitalized with what was later described as a "simple attack of appendicitis."

It was during this attack that the doctors began to express concern for the health of the fetus in her womb. They warned Edi and Alessandro that the baby would most likely be born with a disability and they strongly encouraged them to abort the child. Edi's response demonstrated the steel courage and authentic hope that would serve her well in the challenging years ahead when she vehemently refused to abort the child and carried her son to full term.

The doctors were correct in their concern for the health of the child, and the boy was born with congenital glaucoma. Beginning at the age of six months, the child would endure twenty-seven operations on his eyes.

In a recent interview, Edi shared, "My son was born with a serious illness of the eyes, not well known then, glaucoma. At first doctors saw him and diagnosed him, minimized it. But come daytime, he suffered, he cried. His eyes would become red. We took him to an eye doctor in Torino, professor Galenga, a famous doctor, who gave us the correct diagnosis, a diagnosis with no hope." The prognosis, Edi continues was "As Andrea would grow older he would become blind."

Edi was determined that her son would not be dominated and defined by his blindness. She understood that to pity him would make him pity himself. From the same interview Edi shared the following,

"I decided that if I wanted my son to become a man,

there were no alternatives. There would be no pity. I had to find such strength within myself. It was terrible because it was almost impossible not to feel pain in front of that vivacious young boy like bright silver, with a look becoming more empty every day. With my tears, I would have condemned him to unhappiness. I would have made him a victim, I kept telling myself."

The last ray of sight was taken from Edi's sons eyes when he was struck in the face with a specially made soccer ball designed for the sight impaired. The spikes on the ball pierced his eye and turned out any remaining light. After rushing her son to the hospital and refusing to allow the doctor to remove his cornea, Edi made her way home with her injured son. Edi relates the incident that followed:

"During the trip while I was applying pressure to his eyes, to stop the bleeding, a lady who was looking said 'poor little boy, the poor little boy' to my son. I snapped at her like lightening. 'I permit no one to say poor little boy to my son.' I don't know what that woman must have thought. She probably thought I was a mad woman. But regarding this, I was unapproachable, I have always been like this."

"When I am older, will I see Poldo's house?" was her son's sincere question. Edi's answer to the son she had refused to abort was truthful yet hopeful, "You will never see it, but you will see other things that we are not able to see."

There is little doubt that the world is grateful and owes a debt to this Italian mother who refused to abort her child and raised with excellence one of this generation greatest artistic gifts, Andrea Bochelli.

In every way a mother can, Edi Bochelli acted in courage and instilled in Andre a hope that would not bow to the physical limitation of blindness. Andre has risen to become one of the world's most popular and heralded vocalist.

His mother recognized his passion for music early in his life. While in the hospital a Russian patient in the adjacent room listened to classical music all day long. Edi watched, as her six-month-old son would "not stop banging his feet and turning towards the wall where the music was coming from."

That infant keeping beat to the music with his feet at six months old, began playing the piano when he was six years old. At the encouragement of his parents, he learned to play several other instruments, including the flute, saxophone, guitar, trumpet and drums. His love of music and his thirst for learning was insatiable and continues to this day.

Andrea began to be recognized as a major talent and had his first break at the age of thirty-four when a demo tape found its way into the hands of the great Italian tenor, Luciano Pavarotti. Pavarotti was so impressed with the quality of Andrea's voice, that he invited him to record a duet. The song 'Miserere" became immensely popular throughout Europe.

Since his coming out in 1992, Andre has received over 20 music awards including seven World Music Awards - four for Best Selling Classical Artist and three for Best Selling Italian singer. He has won six Classical Brits Awards and his classical album 'Sacred Arias" is the biggest selling classical album by any solo artist in history.

All the success that has come His way has not altered the character of the man Edi gave her life to shape. Andre is well known for living with the same confidence, serenity, and excellence he displays when standing and performing before thousands of fans in concert.

Andrea is well loved as a musician and as a man and is an inspiration to millions. An Australia woman once wrote to Edi Bochelli, declaring, "I bless you Signora, because you have put Andrea on this earth."

Edi recalls, "We (my husband and I) wanted him to become a man, not a handicapped person." The evidence is in, Edi, you have succeeded. When someone refers to Bocelli's blindness in conversation, it is not unusual for someone to reply with surprise, "Andre Bocelli is blind?"

Andrea, when speaking of his mother's refusal to take the advice of doctors and abort her son has quipped, "The young brave wife decided not to abort, and the child was born. That woman was my mother, and I was the child. Maybe I am partisan, but I can say it was the right choice."

Edi Bocelli, a Hero of hope, who, out of a heartbreaking circumstance, raised and guided a child to have hope for his future and become a man who let nothing stop him from reaching his dream.

Thoughts

The Innkeeper

As she watched her young son play in the dirt outside her family home, this mother and wife reflected on the many blessings of her life. Among them was her marriage to Salmon, a respected prince of Judah. Though not born a Jew, she was adopted into the tribe and given a place of honor among the tribal families. This welcomed acceptance into what was usually a closed society was due to her daring though unexpected role many years before in helping the nation of Israel to acquire the territory in which they now lived.

The boy, Boaz, now chasing the family dog through the date palms that dotted the yard and gave much needed shade to the outdoor living space, was already displaying the qualities of character and strength that would serve him well when fully grown.

Though she had great hope for her son's future and for the generations to follow, she could not have imagined on this day that her Boaz would be known for courageously redeeming a young widow named Ruth; that her great grandson Jessie would father the most respected King in the history of the nation – King David; or that many generations later her seed would produce the man that would be the husband of a young maiden named Mary, the mother of the messiah.

Her early beginnings certainly did not foreshadow the life she was now enjoying, nor predict the legacy that would follow. As she listened to her son's gleeful laughter, her thoughts wandered to the day that seemed like another life a lifetime ago when 2 Jewish spies knocked on the door of Rahab, the harlot, and hope was birthed.

For Rahab, the knock on the door that day certainly did not knowingly predict the radical shift that was going to take place over the next few days. It would not have sounded any different from the many others heard vibrating through her establishment each day. But as she looked on the faces of the two Hebrew men standing in the doorway, she must have had some indication that these men were not the usual customers.

"We were told this is a place where we can find lodging," the two men stated, their accents confirming her suspicion that they were not from Jericho. She hesitated to respond as she processed the evidence in front of her along with all the rumors that had been spreading throughout the city. If these were the men she suspected, then they were dangerous and she must consider her answer carefully.

For several days, the city had been buzzing with rumors of a massive army gathering on the other side of the river. The stories of their past conquests, the miraculous crossing of the Red Sea, and other demonstrations of the power of their God had caused terror in the heart of the people.

Rahab had heard the conversations dominated with talk of impending destruction as she walked through the market place each day. The emotions of everyone in the city including Rahab were on a ragged edge. And now, two men stood in front of her that could be of those who threatened her city, her way of life, and possibly her life itself.

Rahab was filled with apprehension as she considered her response to the men at her door. She was fully aware that it would go against the culture of hospitality that guided their society to refuse them entrance; yet to welcome them might put her and her family's life at risk. She also was sure the ramifications of her decision were far more reaching than she could at the moment calculate. Yet, as she looked into the eyes of the two men awaiting her answer, something inside of her whispered, "hope".

"Come in," she quietly, but resolutely invited, "you are welcome in my house".

The next knock on the door came a few hours later and would challenge her resolve. "Rahab," the serious tenor of the King's emissary's voice and the intimidating presence of the armed men around him made it clear he had not come to socialize. "We have word that there are spies in the city," the man continued without waiting for a reply. "And we believe they've taken up lodging in your house. If this is so, the king demands that you bring them out to us."

Rahab lowered her eyes as she considered the implications of her next words. Should she follow the longing of her heart that was kindled by hopeful expectation? Or did her destiny lie in giving these men what they and the king were demanding? Each choice had its consequence. As she raised her eyes and looked into the intimidating face of the emissary, "hope," whispered again and the resulting courage shaped her response.

"Yes, the men you are referring to did come to me," Rahab stated confidently. "I didn't know who they were or where they came from".

Then Rahab continued her response in a way congruent to her pagan culture where deceit was a tool to be used and truth something to be manipulated, "You may be able to catch them if you hurry for they only stayed a short time and left the city just before the gates closed."

Troubled, but satisfied, the men hurried off and Rahab shut the door behind them. There was a mixture of apprehension and excitement in her spirit now as she walked up the stairs and onto the roof where she had hidden the men. She knew that her world had radically changed. Although she didn't know what it would look like, she was sure that Her path was now set and she would continue to follow the promise of hope that had guided her through this life-changing day.

The story of Rahab recorded in the book of Joshua and later referenced, along with greats like Abraham and Gideon in the Hebrews hall of faith is one of the amazing stories of Biblical history.

We don't know the back-story of Rahab's life, or the circumstances that led her to become an innkeeper of a hostel that provided more than room and board. Scripture doesn't fill in the details, but from what we can learn from the social mores of the time and the place prostitution played in the culture of Jericho, we can be somewhat confident that Rahab was not "living the dream."

Though Rahab provided a service accepted in her society, her lifestyle carried with it a level of shame and rejection that had her living in the shadows with no hope of ever becoming anything more. Honor and respect were out of reach for the harlot of Jericho - until that hope-filled day.

Who would have thought that a woman branded in scripture as "the harlot Rahab" would play a destiny-changing role for her family and a nation and be listed in the lineage of the Messiah? Well, that's the potential for those choosing hope and acting in faith.

Thoughts

The Fourth Passenger

The young black girl of Irish, Scottish and African ancestry stood shaking in fear as she gazed wide-eyed out the window at her father standing with shotgun in hand. Her fear was not provoked by the image of the gun but by the menacing line of clansmen marching past her Montgomery, Alabama home.

That nightmarish image of the KKK in front of her home was indelibly burned into the mind of this great granddaughter of slaves. It, and other defining moments like it, would play a significant role in moving her to the nation-changing decision she would make later in life.

Miss McCauley, as the local barber, Raymond, knew her before their marriage, was now forty-two years of age and worked as a seamstress at the Montgomery Fair Department Store. It was twenty-four days before Christmas, 1955.

It seemed that this December day would move along like most as she boarded the bus to make her usual journey from work to home. She paid her fare and moved to the first row of seats reserved for blacks in the "colored" section. Moving past the 10 rows of seats reserved for "White Only" passengers was nothing new. She could not even count the times she had to swallow the indignity and shame of those brief walks down the aisle.

There had not been a day in Louis McCauley's life that she was not acutely aware of the limiting segregation and fierce racism that leavened the Alabama culture. She often experienced the Jim Crow laws that effectively disenfranchised the black community and had personally witnessed and felt the sting of hurtful and unfair discrimination.

Louis took the seat on the isle and settled in, anticipating a typical bus ride home. But on this day, December 1, 1955, the ride home would be anything but typical, and the events that were about to unfold would leave a mark on her and the nation. Everything went as expected until the bus reached the third stop in front of the Empire Theatre.

Though it was not the law, it was the practice of the bus drivers to demand that the black passengers in the first rows of the "colored" section move back when the white section was filled and give their seats to the white passengers. As the bus Louise McCauley was riding reached the stop in front of the Empire Theatre, several white passengers boarded the bus, finding that the ten rows of seats designated for them were taken.

As usual, the bus driver, James Blake, moved the "colored" section sign behind the row Louise was sitting in and made the expected demand, "Y'all better make it light on yourselves and let me have those seats."

There were four people sitting in the seats Mr. Blake was trying to vacate. At first no one moved. Mr. Blake, losing his patience, became more demanding,

"Let me have these seats." He barked.

Three of those sitting in the contested row gave into the demand, stood up and moved. But on this day, the fourth passenger had put up with this humiliation one time too many; and out of a hope to live in a better world, Rosa Louise McCauley Parks refused to leave the row. Instead of moving back, she slid over to the window seat.

In her autobiography, My Story, Rosa writes:

"People always say that I didn't give up my seat because I was tired, but that isn't true. I was not tired physically, or no more tired than I usually was at the end of a working day. I was not old, although some people have an image of me as being old then. I was forty-two. No, the only tired I was, was tired of giving in."

Rosa Parks was arrested and charged with a violation of the segregation law of the Montgomery city code. She was bailed out later that night. Four days following her arrest, Rosa was found guilty of disorderly conduct and violating a local ordinance. Her trial lasted 30 minutes and she was fined fourteen dollars. That would not be the only price she would pay for her action as she lost her job and received death threats for many years.

Rosa was later quoted as saying: "I only knew that, as I was being arrested, that it was the very last time that I would ever ride in humiliation of this kind."

In a 1992 Radio interview, Rosa Parks recalled:
"I did not want to be mistreated, I did not want to be deprived of a seat that I had paid for. It was just time... there was opportunity for me to take a stand to express the way I felt about being treated in that manner. I had not planned to get arrested. I had plenty to do without having to end up in jail. But when I had to face that decision, I didn't hesitate to do so because I felt that we had endured that too long. The more we gave in, the more we complied with that kind of treatment, the more oppressive it became."

Rosa's arrest set in motion a boycott by black commuters of the buses in Montgomery lasting 382 days. The effect on the bus transit company's finances was significant and forced the city to lift the law requiring segregation on public buses.

Mrs. Parks refusal to move to the back of the bus did more than change the law in Montgomery, Alabama. It would ignite a movement that would reshape the United States and shake the world. It would set off the spark that lit the fire in a young minister of Dexter Avenue Baptist Church named Dr. Martin Luther King Jr.

Dr. King wrote in his book Stride Toward Freedom:

"Actually, no one can understand the action of Mrs. Parks unless he realizes that eventually the cup of endurance runs over, and the human personality cries out, 'I can take it no longer.'"

Her act and the boycott that followed her arrest became the inspiration for the bus boycott that was a key event in the struggle against Apartheid in South Africa. Rosa's efforts were so inspirational to that nations fight for racial equality that she was invited to be one of the honored people to meet Nelson Mandela upon his release from prison in 1994.

Little did forty-two-year-old Rosa know that December day in 1955 that she would one day be awarded the presidential Medal of Freedom from President Bill Clinton in 1996; awarded the highest award of Congress – the Congressional Gold Medal in 1977; and become an icon and leading spokesperson for the civil rights movement the remainder of her life until her death at the age of ninety-two on October 24, 2005.

Could it be that hope is the womb of desperate action and that Heroes of Hope are often birthed in the heat of persecution?

Thoughts

The Evangelist

The young couple and their two children were captivated by the words of the man the people were calling Jesus. He spoke with great kindness yet with such authority. Every word stirred their hunger for true life and left them nearly breathless. They had never heard any one speak truth like this man.

It had been a long day, however, and the children were becoming hungry. They had come onto the mountain on a whim, by an invitation of a stranger, not thinking to bring along anything to eat. As they contemplated what to do about their lunch, they heard a sound coming from the rest of the crowd scattered on the hillside. It was the sound of surprised wonder at what they could only describe as a miracle.

The family stared in astonishment as they witnessed Jesus breaking several loaves and a few small fish and handing them to his key followers. They watched as each time he touched the food, it multiplied until there was more than enough for everyone.

When one of Jesus' followers handed the father his meal, he

could contain his emotions no longer. He turned to the man sitting near him who he had met just a few hours before, and with tears streaming down his face declared, "We will never be able to thank you enough for inviting us here today. Our lives will never be the same." He then inquired, "Did you know this could happen?"

The man that had invited them responded, "I have to admit that even after all I've witnessed and experienced over the last several months, I was not expecting what we just observed. I'm not surprised, but I am once again astounded."

The family and the man who had invited them stood in preparation to return home as the crowd began to break up and Jesus and his disciples moved toward the boat that would take them to their next assignment. The wife, however, having heard the inviters response, wanted to know more. "You said you have experienced many other things." She began, "Please tell us what you were referring to. We want to hear your story."

The man didn't even hesitate for the story would never be old to him. As he began to speak, he lowered himself back down on the ground and the father and mother settled on the grass and gathered their young children onto their laps.

"I think it important", he began, "that I give you some background so you can understand the significance of all I will tell you. So, let me take you back to the beginning. No, not the day of my birth, but the day I was born again.

The father and mother looked at each other curiously. What had become an unbelievable day was about to become even more so.

"It's impossible to adequately describe to you the torment of my life in what seems now like a lifetime ago. For as long as I can remember, I was driven by voices and tortured by evil forces. I never knew a moment of peace or rest.

"There was a time when those in my community tried to help but to no avail. The anger inside of me became so great I would run through the streets of the city, terrorizing those who had once been my family and friends. I became so dangerous that the only thing they knew to do was chain my hands and feet in order to contain my rage. The demons inside me fueled my strength, and I easily broke free.

"The pain of hurting those I had once loved and the hellish anguish of constant demonic torment drove me to live in the tombs outside the city. The hewn caves now abandoned, except for others like me, became my protection from the elements. I lived naked as I could not tolerate the feel of clothing on my skin, and I often accosted those that traveled through my domain."

The family stared in disbelief at the man, finding it difficult to equate the person being described with the man sitting in front of them. The narrator noticed their confusion, smiled knowingly, and continued with his story.

"Then one day Jesus came and landed on the shore near my

hiding place. I was prepared to perpetrate on him the evil I had visited on so many others who dared come near me. I was, however, not prepared for the battle over life and destiny that was about to explode into my world.

"As Jesus approached me, every resident demon did its worst to keep me from going to him. They knew who he was and screamed inside my head for me to run the opposite direction and to find the protection of the caves. The tearing pain in my chest was unbearable. It was then that an unexplainable flicker of hope rose up though the demonic torment, and I was relentlessly drawn by the love radiating from this man. For the first time in more years than I can remember, I believed something good was possible and I ran to Jesus - not to harass him, but to worship him.

Even as I fell at his feet to worship, fear so gripped me I cried out 'I beg you, do not torment me.' Then Jesus asked my name and I couldn't get the words out before the demons inside me, now more fearful than I, answered, 'My name is Legion, for we are many.' Now that I think of that moment, I'm not sure I even remembered my given name. I had become a fearful, hateful, tormented, hopeless and nameless creature."

Deep emotion marked the faces of the parents as they gathered their children closer on their laps. The story was touching them in very personal ways. They, too, had begun to feel the pale of hopelessness resident in the difficult circumstances of their own lives. They listened even more intently as the man continued his narrative.

"The rest of what happened in the few seconds that followed is not clear to me," said the man as if reliving the moment. "All I know is that in one instant I was released from every tormenting possessive spirit and for the first time I could remember, I was liberated and thinking clearly. Peace overwhelmed me and I collapsed onto the ground in utter relief. One of the disciples kindly clothed me with borrowed clothing and Jesus came and sat next to me. I can't describe to you the absolute contentment that flooded every part of my world in that moment."

The man and his audience of four sat in silence for a few moments, before he began again.

"You can imagine how disappointed I was when Jesus said he had to go to another region. He said I couldn't go with him but he instructed me to go home to my friends and tell everyone what had happened. Though I wished to go with him, His words filled me with purpose, and I knew I'd been commissioned into my destiny.

"You see friends, you aren't the first to be invited by me to meet Jesus," the man said, addressing the family. "It was difficult returning to the scene of my crimes and facing up to the one-time friends and family that I'd so badly violated. But many of those on this hill today came because they heard my story, saw my transformation and believed."

The man stopped his narrative, stood to his feet and turned toward the sea in time to see Jesus and his disciples enter their boat and push off from the shore. In a voice barely audible by the family, the man declared, "I will live the rest of my life loving and following that man."

The father and mother, now visibly shaken by the story they had heard, followed the man's gaze. They were speechless with gratitude, thankful that a man once known as the demoniac had introduced them to Jesus, and in so doing introduced hope back into their lives.

The Bible doesn't give us a name for this once tormented man. He is only referred to as a man "with an unclean spirit"; a "demon-possessed" man; and a man "who had demons for a long time." He is most often referred to as the Demoniac. I would suggest that his true heavenly identity and assigned calling was "The Evangelist."

Mark, in his account of this story, records that this man, following the instructions of Jesus, not only declared what Jesus had done in his hometown but also into the region known as Decapolis. Decapolis was an area embracing ten cities and several smaller villages. The impact of his witness in this region is evident in the welcome Jesus received when he returned to the area and the huge crowds that followed after him, setting up the context of this story - the miracle of the feeding of the four thousand.

From demoniac to evangelist; from a lost cause, to a man with a cause; from demon possessed to love possessed; from a slave of hell to a hero of hope. This is the transformation possible for the person who in one defining moment, chooses to be captivated by the expectation of good.

Thoughts

The Politician

As William lay consumed by the influenza that had so often come upon him, he had much to think on as his mind traveled over the length of his nearly 74 years of life. Though it had been a full and satisfying lifetime he couldn't help but reflect with some regret on his early years as a foolish and self-centered son of a wealthy merchant.

He had enrolled in St. Josephs College at Cambridge, yet remained absorbed in the partying and gambling scene so prevalent in his level of society. Thinking on those days he concluded, "As much pains were taken to make me idle as were ever taken to make me studious."

William's lack of interest in his studies was matched by his lack of concern for the society he lived in. He did, however, have some ambitions in life: winning election to Parliament in 1780 at the age of twenty-one. Even in Parliament, he remembered being less than engaged in the potential good his position offered. In his more philosophical moments he would admit, "The first years in Parliament I did nothing – nothing to any purpose. My own distinction was my darling object."

It was not that he was blind to the world around him; he just had little interest in those less fortunate. Even the plight of the slaves he would often observe in daily life did little to stir his compassion. The fact that slavery and the slave trade were deeply entrenched in the culture of the late 1700's in Great Britain gave him justification for his lack of concern.

William was aware that English traders were capturing between thirty-five and fifty thousand Africans a year and shipping them across the Atlantic to be enslaved in British colonies. It was major business and had become an economic necessity; at least, that is what William had become convinced of. What could one man, he maintained, hope to accomplish when pitted against such a monstrous political and economic machine?

Those were the values that determined this mans' thinking and direction until Easter Sunday morning in the year 1789. On that day, the young man, who had disclaimed any belief in God and believed he had no responsibility for others, was confronted with the Gospel of Christ.

That moment for William was more than just the acceptance of a good thought, but the full embrace of the good news that led to personal transformation.   It was then he rejected his agnostic beliefs, welcomed Jesus as the truth, and William Wilberforce started down the road to becoming the central voice to abolish slavery in his part of the world.

William once wrote, "So enormous, so dreadful, so

irremediable did the trade's wickedness appear that my own mind was completely made up for abolition. Let the consequences be what they would: I from this time determined that I would never rest until I had effected its abolition." On another occasion he is known to have stated, "You may choose to look the other way but you can never say again that you did not know."

Now, many years and hundreds of fiercely fought political and spiritual battles later William lay on his bed, burning with fever, knowing he was coming to the end of his life on earth. Those who knew him best, found it difficult to believe that he once lived with such indifference to the plight of those he would later spend his life working to set free.

And now, was it possible, he wondered, that the cause he had fought for so long was about to be realized? Should he hope to believe that the news he had just received was true? The note held frailly in his hand stated that the bill to abolish slavery throughout the British Empire was at this moment being presented for guaranteed passage in the House of Lords! Could it be that the dream he had so unwaveringly hoped for was now about to be a reality?

As the truth of this potential breakthrough set in, joy began to overwhelm the pain of his illness, and he smiled with holy satisfaction at hope realized. Three days later William Wilberforce breathed his last. One month after his death the House of Lords passed the *Slavery Abolition Act*, abolishing slavery in most of the British Empire.

William Wilberforce was not the only one fighting for the abolition of slavery. He was inspired by and partnered with people like William Pitt, a future prime minister, and the abolitionists Thomas Clarkson, Granville Sharp and Hanna More. Wilberforce however, is recognized as the voice and uncompromising force behind the movement.

As a Member of Parliament William wholeheartedly engaged in the fight. He once wrote, "We are too young to realize that certain things are impossible... So we will do them anyway."

He introduced his first anti-slavery bill in the House of Commons on April 18, 1791 with great optimism. Here are some excerpts of his presentation speech:

> "Let us not despair; it is a blessed cause, and success, ere long, will crown our exertions... let us persevere and our triumph will be complete. Never, never will we desist till we have wiped away this scandal... looking back to the history of these enlightened times, (posterity) will scarce believe that it has been suffered to exist so long a disgrace and dishonour to this country."

Little did William realize the truth of his words and the size of the task before him. His first anti-slavery bill was defeated 163 to 88. He didn't give up, however, and presented anti-slavery bills in years 1792, 1793, 1797, 1798, 1799, 1801, and 1805. Pro-slavery forces defeated each of these bills so fiercely that many friends were fearful for Williams' safety.

Wilberforce, however, lived in the desperation of hope and never stopped his crusade. On February 23, 1807, having been passed by the House of Lords, the *Slave Trade Act of 1807* was presented to the House of Commons with tribute to Wilberforce and was passed 283 votes to 16. It is said that William stood unashamedly in awe, with tears streaming down his face.

The Slave Trade Act of 1807, though an important victory, was only half the battle. The act made it illegal to engage in the slave trade but did not abolish existing slavery. Therefore, Wilberforce continued to advance the cause even after leaving Parliament due to poor health in 1826.

Wilberforce made his last anti-slavery speech in April of 1833. A month later the Bill for the Abolition of Slavery was presented and passed on August 28, 1833.

William Wilberforce was buried in Westminster Abby in recognition of his tenacious spirit and historic accomplishments. In 1840, a seated statue of William was erected, commemorating his life-long labor to abolish slavery.

The following summarizes the heart of a man that was an authentic hero of hope:

"Accustom yourself to look first to the dreadful consequences of failure; then fix your eye on the glorious prize which is before you; and when your strength begins to fail, and your spirits are well-nigh exhausted, let the animating view rekindle your resolution, and call forth in renewed vigour the fainting energies of your soul."
— *William Wilberforce)*

Thoughts

The Steadfast Surgeon

"Doctor, the patient has died." Joseph Lister, the attending physician slumped into the chair outside the children's ward. He had heard that statement more times than he could count. Too many patients were surviving the surgery only to die a few days or weeks later of ward fever. This last patient was a young boy with a compound fracture of the leg. Though the bone had broken the skin, the surgery to set the leg was not complicated. Now the boy was dead. There was no understandable reason for his young life to have been cut short.

As Joseph walked out of the patient ward to find a solitary place to think and pray, he quietly but resolutely declared, "Something has to be done to stop these senseless deaths." It was often that Joseph, a Quaker, found his peace and direction through quiet contemplation. It was his way of submitting his scientific mind to the wisdom of his maker.

In spite of the opposition he knew would come from both the medical and scientific communities, Joseph began his journey to discover the answer that would stop the death of nearly half the surgery patients in the Edinburgh Hospital where he worked.
After several months of observation and experimentation,

Joseph invited a fellow surgeon and the professor of Clinical surgery in Edinburgh University, James Syme, to visit him in his study on the grounds of the hospital. He wanted to share with a friend some of his conclusions and beliefs about the cause of ward fever before presenting it to the broader medical community.

"I'm convinced", Joseph cautiously began his conversation with his colleague, "that what we have assumed about sepsis is flawed." Seeing the intrigue on his friend's face gave him courage to continue. "Could it be that the cause is not from inside the wound, or surgical opening, but is coming from the outside?" The look on his colleague's countenance changed from intrigue to concern and skepticism.

"Joseph", his colleague began, "it is universally accepted around the world that infection arises spontaneously within a wound, making it virtually impossible to eliminate it." Joseph's fellow surgeon continued to argue his point. "As difficult as it may be, we must accept that this is always going to be the case with open wounds, rather they occur from accident or surgery."

"I will not accept that as fact." Joseph now warming to his conviction. "There has to be an answer. If we believe there is nothing we can do to oppose this tragic waste of life, we have no real hope to offer the people we have taken an oath to heal."

Joseph continued his argument by reminding his friend of what they both already knew. "As a medical community, we have been able to solve two of the great barriers that for generations stood in the way of effective surgery. The first was the problem of uncontrolled bleeding that led to patient deaths. As you will remember from your own student studies, the work of Ambroise Pare, the French doctor. In 1552 he developed a way to tie off the ends of blood vessels with thread, minimizing bleeding.

"The second limiting problem confronting the surgeon in the past," Joseph reminded his friend, "was the pain level of the patients. We had to operate as quickly as possible, trying to limit the agony brought on by the surgery. It wasn't that long ago, my friend, in fact, while you and I were still university students, that anesthetics were first introduced. This solution gave men like you and me time to be effective in our surgery and improve our techniques."

Leaning forward on the edge of his chair holding up three fingers to emphasize his point, Joseph passionately rose to the occasion. "If we can solve the issue of excessive bleeding," He stated, touching his ring finger and bending it into his fist. "And we can find the solution to the patient's pain," now touching and bending his middle finger into his fist. "Then," holding up his remaining index finger, Joseph spoke with pronounced emphasis, "why can we not find the answer to this last barrier to successful healing of surgical patients?"

A tense quiet filled the room for several seconds as the two men stared at each other. The surgeon was the first to break the silence. "I understand your concern Joseph and appreciate your passion," he softly responded. He then stood slowly and began to pace around the room in increasing annoyance. "But there's no evidence for what you are proposing."

This was the opening for which Joseph was waiting. Over the last several months he had been preparing himself to answer the very argument posed by his surgeon friend. "Not true," Joseph enthusiastically exclaimed. "I am confident that there is evidence that suggests exactly what I believe to be true. And", he continued bravely, "if I am correct, I believe I have a solution to the problem."

As a scientist and doctor, Joseph's friend, could not resist being intrigued by Josephs claim. "I find it hard to believe, Joseph, though I believe you to be a fine doctor and recognized scientist, that you have discovered what others have been unable to. However," the surgeon conceded as he walked back and lowered himself into the chair he had vacated, "I will listen to what you have to say."

Joseph began his defense with a personal anecdote. "My father, among other things, was a wine maker. He often complained about the problem of the wine going bad because of faulty fermentation. We couldn't find the cause of the spoilage until we came across Louis Pasteur's work in this area. Pasteur proved that the problem did not come from organisms spontaneously coming to life inside the wine, but came from germs that enter from the outside air. This made me consider that the cause of infection may also come from outside a wound."

Joseph then shared his observations of patients with simple fractures and those with compound fractures. He had observed that patients with simple fractures recovered well and those with compound fractures often died after the bones were set successfully. "I believe," Joseph surmised, "that the wound caused by the compound fracture exposed the patient to infection from germs introduced into the wound from the outside. If this is true, then we can attack the germs and prevent deaths from infection."

James was beginning to waver in his commitment to the status quo, but had many questions to ask his friend before being convinced. Joseph and his friend sat for the next two hours debating the issues. It was then professor James asked his friend, "You mentioned that if this is true, you believe you have the solution. What is it?"

Knowing his solutions might be as controversial and as his premise, Joseph leaned back in his chair and shared his plan. "I have already begun to implement two procedures that have shown amazing results. Before every surgery I wash my hands and put on clean clothes." Joseph could see his friend wrestling internally with the arguments against what he was proposing, yet, he continued. "Then I sterilize all my surgical instruments and the bandages used in the operation with carbolic acid. In doing these two things we kill the germs before they are allowed into the wound."

The professor sat quietly for several moments. The turmoil inside of himself consisted of more than the lingering resistance to Joseph's proposal. His greatest concern was for his friend's career and reputation.

"Joseph," James voice revealed his anxiety. "Let me first address your theory. You must know that many of those in the medical profession do not believe that germs exist. They have a hard time accepting that there is something real that cannot be seen. You must also realize that doctors are often so busy doing what they have always done they don't believe they have the time or need to consider anything new."

James, taking a deep breath continued. "Now let me speak to your methods. Surgeons believe that a blood spotted apron gives the patience confidence that the doctor has experience. They will be very slow to give up something they see as a benefit to their patients and, frankly, something they hold as a status symbol. Their resistance will only increase as they find your sterilization procedure time consuming, monotonous, and costly."

James looked directly into his friend's eyes and began to plead. "Joseph, you and I have been colleagues for many years and I have watched you grow into a fine doctor and researcher. So, as your friend, I implore you to think carefully. If you publish your thesis, you will be strongly opposed by some of the most highly respected physicians in the world. You will be ridiculed by those wishing to maintain the status quo and protect their own reputations. It is even possible, my friend, that you will lose your position and have your reputation destroyed by the fierce opposition you may face. I implore you, Joseph, count the cost."

Joseph reflected for a moment on the gravity of James words and then remembered the tragic death of that young man with the broken leg. With his resolve set he responded to his dear friend. "Thank you, James, for your concern for my life and future. You have always shown great care for me. Believe me James, I do comprehend the opposition I will face in presenting my beliefs and procedures. But James, the controversy and the opposition are none of my concern." Then leaning toward his colleague, Joseph concluded, "My concern is the welfare and life of my patients."

The dialogue between Dr. Joseph Lister and Professor James Syme is fictional. It is not, however in my opinion, beyond the realm of possibility as these two men were long time colleagues and would have certainly had conversations on the subject of this narrative. I am also confident that Professor Syme, Joseph Lister's mentor, would have warned Joseph of the opposition he would face.

What is not fictional is that Joseph Lister did face tremendous opposition to his controversial premise and procedures. Lister, however, never yielded to the ridicule, and the results of his work were astounding. Those who followed Lister's procedures in Munich, Germany lowered the death rate caused by infection after surgery from 80% to almost zero. In spite of these results, it took twelve years from the publishing of Dr. Lister's papers in 1867 for his system of sterilization to be widely accepted. Ironically, the last group of physicians to accept the validity of Lister's methods were the doctors of his own nation, England.

Dr. Lister received many awards and recognitions during his lifetime. Among them, he was dubbed Sir Joseph Lister by Queen Victoria. But for the man who believed he was directed in life by God, his greatest rewards are the countless lives saved by his steadfast pursuit of something greater.

The road to bringing hope to those most in need, is usually not a clear path, but one with opposing forces. Dr. Joseph Lister is a Hero of Hope for believing that what has always been accepted need not always be.

Thoughts

The Orphan's Allies

Hegai watched as his friend was berated by the King's overseer and knew this would not end well. It was the king's command that all the servants were to bow in reverence when the overseer passed through the gates of the city. Yet for several days this man, known to be a Jew, refused to be intimidated and would not bow or give him notice. The overseer of all the Kings princes, Haman was not accustomed to being resisted.

It was evident to Hegai that on this day Haman had reached the end of his patience and would act to destroy the servant. Little did Hegai know, however, that the overseer had bigger plans then the destruction of just one Jew. "Before I'm done," Haman spoke through clenched teeth to his confidential secretary as they withdrew from the confrontation, "this man's rebellion will bring the destruction of every Jew found in the king's realm."

As Hegai, a eunuch in service to the King, stood thinking on this heated conversation, he remembered the first time he saw the Jew that would become his friend and ally. It was before Haman was the king's overseer and shortly after the king had ordered the beautiful virgins to be gathered and prepared as candidates to be his queen.

Hegai had watched as the man he would one day learn was the Jew Mordecai, walked past the palace walls and approached the guard at the king's harem. He viewed with curiosity as the man engaged the guard in conversation. Hegai, having been put in charge of the king's virgins had a growing concern about this man's activity. After several days of the same activity Hegai knew it was time to discover the meaning of the Jews inquiry.

Upon questioning the guard, Hegai learned that the Jew had daily inquired of the welfare of one of the young virgins, a woman named Hadassah. This greatly intrigued Hegai because he too had noticed Hadassah above all the other beautiful women being prepared to be presented to the king. He had been so captivated by her that he had placed her in the finest apartment in the harem, given her seven specially chosen maids to assist her, and was personally involved in her purification and preparation.

"Who is this Jew" Hegai pondered, "and why does he have such great interest in my favored virgin?" A suspicion began to grow in Hegai that this man was connected to Hadassah in a way that could threaten his hope for her future.

Mordecai, the Jew in question, had noticed the king's eunuch observing him from time to time, but was more concerned about the welfare of Hadassah, his adopted daughter, than the curiosity of the man. Mordecai, like many others of his nation, had been taken from Jerusalem and led into captivity and now lived in exile in a strange land. It was in this land that his uncle and aunt had died, leaving his cousin without parents. Mordecai adopted Hadassah and raised her as his own until the day the king's men showed up at his door and took her away.

Even though Mordecai had gained favor and acquired a position as an attendant in the king's court, he well knew that living in Shushan, the capital city of the Persian Empire, held some disadvantages for those of Jewish decent. To protect Hadassah from discrimination he had instructed her to not reveal her nationality. Ever since Hadassah had been taken from him and placed with the other virgins to be groomed for the king's selection, Mordecai was captivated by the hope that Hadassah was chosen by God to play an important role in the destiny of his people.

It had been nearly one year since Hadassah, now named Esther by the nation of her captivity, had been taken from Mordecai. One year of Mordechai daily going to the guard of the harem and asking about his daughter's welfare. It was a year in which Hegai faithfully and meticulously prepared Esther for her future. In that year, Mordechai and Hegai became friends with a common interest and goal – to prepare Esther for her night with the king, and her date with destiny.

It was the custom for the virgin designated for a given night, having had a year of preparation, to be taken from the women's quarter and presented to the King. Following a night in the bed of the king, the woman would either be chosen queen or be immediately taken to the house of the concubines. In the possibility that she would not be selected, the virgin was allowed to gather anything she desired from the place of her preparation to benefit her in her life time in the king's concubine.

Hegai and Mordechai knew the time had come when Esther would be led into the Kings chamber. They also knew that after that one night, Hegai's charge and Mordechai's daughter would either be shut away in the harem for the rest of her life, or be chosen as the new queen.

"Esther," Hegai began as he gave her his final instruction before she left the women's quarter to go to the king, "do not take anything but what I advise you to take." After hearing Hegai's instruction and hearing his list of things that were to go with her, Esther looked at him with a puzzled expression.

Before she could speak Hegai continued, "I know, Esther, this will not provide well for your future if you are not chosen and it risks you presenting yourself as arrogant. But I believe", he quietly but confidently stated, "it will not offend the king, but rather cause him to be intrigued by you right from the start. I'm asking you to trust me one more time."

Esther had learned to trust this man that had watched over her so diligently in the last year and was willing to trust again. She collected her things, embraced her mentor, and started toward the king's chambers.

Hegai, the king's eunuch, a descendant of Hezekiah, the King of Judah, and Mordecai, an exile of the tribe of Benjamin loved the same young woman. They had done what each of them could to prepare Esther for her night with the king. Holding her in hope, the two friends stood outside the King's chamber, awaiting the king's decision. They would not be disappointed.

The story of Esther, recorded in the book by the same name, is a complicated and intriguing one that would make a fascinating novel. As you are aware, Haman put his plan into place to destroy the Jews and Mordecai countered with his. Esther become the key figure in determining which plan would succeed.

Mordecai convinced Esther to put her life at risk, approach the king without his summons, and activate the plan that would result in the hanging death of Haman, the advancement of Mordecai, and the saving of a nation. Wow, what a story!

The rest of the story of this Hero of Hope narrative, however, is found in the story before the story. Some of what I will share now is conjecture based on Biblical and historic investigation that cannot be directly proven. However, I find the connections compelling enough to share them here.

The conflict between Haman and Mordecai, briefly mentioned at the beginning of this narrative was an historic one dating back to the time of King Saul. It was at the time Saul was establishing his kingdom that God instructed him to destroy all the Amalikites. The intended destruction of the Amalikites was the result of the way they had ambushed Israel during their exodus from Egypt.

Saul, fearing the people, did not follow the instructions of the Lord and spared the King of the Amalkites, King Agag. Samuel the prophet, upon discovering Saul's failure, followed through with the command of the Lord and killed the King. Saul's failure, however, cost Saul his kingship and set up the conflict decades later between Haman and Mordecai that nearly caused the extinction of the nation of Israel.

Haman, the king's overseer, the man that plotted the death of Mordecai and the destruction of the Jews is referred to as an Agagite, identifying him as a descendant of King Agag – the King Saul was to destroy. It seems evident that Saul did not completely destroy the household of King Agag, but left a remnant whose descendant was Haman.

It is no coincidence that God prepared Mordecai, a Benjamite, to stop the generational destruction a Benjamite began. In standing up against Haman, Mordechai fulfilled prophetic destiny as a descendant of Benjamin, declared by his ancestor, Israel. As Israel was about to die he prophesied over each of his sons. Over Benjamin, Israel proclaimed the words that Mordecai would live up to: "Benjamin is a ravenous wolf, devouring his enemies in the morning and dividing his plunder in the evening."

The character of Hegai, the eunuch that prepared Esther for her debut with the king is also of historic nature, finding its story in the time of King Hezekiah found in II Kings chapter 20. At a time when the King was deathly ill, Isaiah, the prophet, told Hezekiah that he was to prepare his household for his impending death. The King plead with God in prayer, and the Lord answered through Isaiah, giving Hezekiah fifteen more years of life. God validated his promise by causing the shadow of the sun to go ten degrees backward.

It was then that the King became proud and displayed arrogantly all the treasures of Israel to the son of the King of Babylon. This act of arrogance and lack of wisdom brought another promise, a dark promise, to the King through the prophet Isaiah:

"The time is coming when everything in your palace, all the treasures stored up by your ancestors until now, will be carried off to Babylon. And some of your descendants, your own flesh and blood who will be born to you, will be taken away, and they will become eunuchs in the palace of the King of Babylon.

King Hezekiah's response forms one of the saddest statements of scripture: "The word of the Lord you have spoken is good." For he thought, "Will there not be peace and security in my lifetime."

The failure of King Hezekiah to repent left the next generation of male offspring barren. It is not too far of a stretch to believe that Hegai, the eunuch that prepared Esther for her destiny, was one of these men. If so, it demonstrates the redemptive nature of God in using the result of a tragedy to help save a nation.

It is in the book of Esther that these historic narratives come together in a Hollywood like climax. The good guys win; the bad guy loses, and a nation is rescued from annihilation. More than that, it is a beautiful picture of the power of God to redeem man's failures, keep his promises to his people, and choose Heroes of Hope to carry out his plans.

Thoughts

Bibliography

The Accountant
Oskar Schindler, His list for Life
www.oskarschindler.com, Louis Bülow
Privacy ©2015-17
Oskar Schindler – The Riddle of an Enigma. Michael Demtschyna
http://www.michaeldvd.com.au/Articles/Who IsOskarSchindler/WhoIsOskarSchindler.html

The Secret Son
Holy Bible: Exodus 1,2

The Conductor
Harriet Tubman: http://harriettubman.com
Biography.com
https://www.biography.com/people/harriet-tubman-9511430#!
Harriet Tubman, Wikipedia, the free encyclopedia
https://en.wikipedia.org/wiki/Harriet_Tubman
Underground Railroad, Wikipedia, the free encyclopedia
https://en.wikipedia.org/wiki/Underground_Railroad

The Young Mill Worker
Stanley Meets Livingstone, by Martin Dugard, Smithsonian Magazine October 2003 wwwsmithonianmag.com
Henry Morton Stanley, Wikipedia, the free encyclopedia
https://www.goodreads.com/author/quotes/191362.William_Wilberforce
David Livingston, Wikipedia, the free encyclopedia

https://en.wikipedia.org/wiki/David_Livingstone
David Livingstone, www.biographyonline.net

The Governor
Holy Bible: Nehemiah 1-17

The Young Brave Wife
Edi Bochelli's Story, RioCities.com
The "I am Whole Life" project YouTube video;
LifeSiteNews.com
Andrea Bocelli Biography; TheFamousPeople.com Updated
July 30, 2017
https://www.thefamouspeople.com/profiles/andrea
-bocelli-4609.php

The Innkeeper
Holy Bible: Joshua 2; Ruth 4:21; Matthew 1:5; Hebrews 11;
James 2:25

The fourth Passenger
Biography Online:
http://www.biographyonline.net/humanitarian/rosa-
parks.html
Philadelphia Martin Luther King, Jr. Association for non-
violence: Rosa L Parks
http://www.philadelphiamlk.org/Pages/RosaParks.as
px
Parks, Rosa (1992). "Main Reason For Keeping Her Seat".
"Parks Recalls Bus Boycott, Excerpts from an interview with
Lynn Neary" (radio interview).

Interview with Lynn Neary. National Public Radio. Archived from the original on December 1, 2014.

The Evangelist
Holy Bible: Matthew 8:28-34; Mark 5:1-20; 7:31-8:1-13; Luke 8:26-39

The Politician
William Wilberfrce, Antislavery politician, Christianity Today
http://www.christianitytoday.com/history/people/activists/william-wilberforce.html
William Wilberforce quotes 2016 Goodreads inc.
https://www.goodreads.com/author/quotes/191362.William_Wilberforce
William Wilberforce, Wikipedia
https://en.wikipedia.org/wiki/William_Wilberforce

The Steadfast Surgeon
Father of Modern Surgery. Ann Lamont, 1992
https://answersingenesis.org/creation-scientists/joseph-lister-father-of-modern-surgery/
Joseph Lister: Famous Scientists.
https://www.famousscientists.org/joseph-lister/

The Orphans Allie
Holy Bible: Esther 1-10; I Samuel 15; II Kings 20:17-19

A special note of appreciation to The Blue Letter Bible for its assistance in providing tools for researching scripture and historical background on Biblical characters.

About the Author

David Crone and his wife, Deborah, are the Senior Leaders of a community of believers called The Mission in Vacaville, California. They have been in full-time vocational ministry for over 45 years and have served at The Mission for over 25 years. While at The Mission, they helped transition a local church into a global ministry that provides resources for their region and the nations. Their value for team ministry has developed a culture of strong leaders, some of who serve with David and Deborah on the core leadership team of The Mission. Their lives and ministry are known for authenticity, a passion for God's presence, and a pursuit of His kingdom on Earth.

David is a director of the Mission School of Supernatural, a ministry of The Mission, and, along with Deborah, serves on the teaching staff of the school. In partnership with The Mission, NIS Ventures, and Kingdom Development Group of Australia, David has developed supernatural training schools in the Philippines and Fiji. He serves as the International Director of Mission Fiji and Deeper Life, Philippines.

David and Deborah have traveled extensively, ministering in 23 nations. David is the author of five books. Deborah, an accomplished artist and designer works as the project Manager at The Mission, having overseen 100,000 square feet of building remodeling. David and Deborah are welcomed speakers at conferences and churches both at home and overseas.

David's Latest Release!

21 Days of Hope

A companion book to Prisoner of Hope and Heroes of Hope.

21 days of hope is more than a book you read. It is designed to take you on a journey that will move you from ineffective wishing to empowered hoping and release you from being held hostage to circumstances so you can become a joyful prisoner of hope.

Great for Small Group Study

21 Days of Hope is easily used for a small-group experience. Taking one or two days of hope each week, the group leader can encourage dialogue on the day's thought, the individual's experience in the activations, and revelations gained from their Bible meditations. In this way, with the addition of the participants praying for each other, small groups should experience both hopeful expectation and healthy community.

Other Books by David Crone

PRISONER OF HOPE
FOREWORD BY KRIS VALLOTTON

In Prisoner of Hope David Crone lays out a powerful argument for the importance of choosing hope and living with a confident expectation of the goodness of God. David speaks from life experiences that have challenged the validity of a hopeful existence and reveals the keys to defeating those negative circumstances. Prisoner of Hope is not a book of theory or cold theology, but a breathing epistle of the authentic value of living in expectation. In reading this book you will re-discover your childlike faith and your heart will be freshly tuned to the life giving sound of hope.

DECLARATIONS THAT EMPOWER US
FOREWORD BY KRIS VALLOTTON

Declarations That Empower Us is a training manual for anyone wanting to partner with heaven for personal or corporate breakthrough. These declarations are dedicated to transforming our minds so that we can view life through God's eternal perspectives, and bring hope to this desperate and dying planet. Every Christian needs to read this book! Without question, this book will change your thinking and transform the world around you. Some of the declarations in this book are already bringing life and hope to individuals and church communities in many places throughout the United States and in several countries.

DECISIONS THAT DEFINE US
FOREWORD BY BILL JOHNSON

The message that will change the world is only as strong as the transformation that has first taken place within believers. In Decisions that Define Us, David Crone documents his personal and corporate journey of transformation as senior leader of a transitioning church in Northern California. Each decision in this book represents the spoils of a battle fought and costly kingdom lesson learned by this leader, his team, and their local fellowship. Within these pages you will be challenged and inspired to pursue God's Kingdom at any cost and to discover practical ways of expressing the supernatural in your own life.

THE POWER OF YOUR LIFE MESSAGE
FOREWORD BY BILL JOHNSON

Author David Crone shares his deeply personal journey experiences that ended with an intimate relationship with His heavenly Father. You will be challenge to change your mindset, which opens the door to internal transformation. You will learn how to define your life message and how to make decisions that lead to fulfilling God's exhilarating and exciting plans for your current and eternal destiny.

Books can be purchased at
www.imissionchurch.com or www.amazon.com

COMING SOON!

More of David's 21 Days book series

21 DAYS OF FAITH

21 days of love

Watch for release dates on Facebook and davecrone.com

53720559R00079

Made in the USA
San Bernardino, CA
26 September 2017